HAIR-RAISING HALLOWEEN

EYE-POPPING
JACK-O'-LANTERNS
DIY GLARES, STARES, AND MORE

by Mary Meinking

CAPSTONE PRESS
a capstone imprint

Blazers Books are published by Capstone Press,
1710 Roe Crest Drive, North Mankato, Minnesota 56003
www.mycapstone.com

Library of Congress Cataloging-in-Publication data
Library of Congress Cataloging-in-Publication data is available on the
Library of Congress website.
ISBN 978-1-5435-3032-2 (library binding)
ISBN 978-1-5435-3036-0 (paperback)
ISBN 978-1-5435-3090-2 (eBook PDF)

Editorial Credits
Mandy Robbins, editor; Juliette Peters, designer;
Morgan Walters, media researcher; Tori Abraham, production specialist;
Marcy Morin, scheduler; Sarah Schuette, photo stylist

Photo Credits
All photos by Capstone Studio: Karon Dubke
Shutterstock: Natykach Nataliia (pumpkin seeds) design element
throughout, Sasa Prudkov, cover, design element throughout, Wandeaw,
cover, design element throughout

Printed and bound in the United States of America.
PA017

Table of Contents

LET THE GUTS FLY!

Do you want to make a truly memorable jack-o'-lantern? Dig in and let the pumpkin guts fly! These fantastically freaky jack-o'-lanterns are sure to impress.

Tip:

Pumpkin carvers use sharp knives and tools. Get an adult to help you with these projects.

PRO CARVING TIPS

To get the most out of
your pumpkins, start
with these carving tips.

Don't let your pumpkins freeze. Bring them inside a few hours before you're ready to carve.

Wash the pumpkins with dish soap. Dry them with an old towel. Be careful not to knock off the stems.

Use a pencil to draw on your designs before you start carving.

Use a pumpkin carving tool kit to carve your creations. You can also use a clay sculpting loop. Get an adult's help with these sharp tools.

Remove the pumpkin guts with a large spoon or flat ice cream scoop.

Use battery-powered candles or glow sticks to light your creations.

Tip:

To preserve your carved pumpkin, ask an adult to spray it with bleach-based cleaner. Spray all the cut surfaces, insides, and the lid. This will keep bugs, mold, and animals away.

GLOWING ALIEN

Look out! An alien has landed on your doorstep.

WHAT YOU NEED:

- ❏ a green squash
- ❏ carving tools
- ❏ a marker
- ❏ 2 pipe cleaners
- ❏ drill
- ❏ green glow sticks

1. Turn the **squash** so that the large bulb is at the top.

2. Cut an opening in the bottom. Remove its guts.

3. Draw on the face. Cut out large eyes and a small, straight mouth. Have an adult drill holes for the nose.

4. Twist the pipe cleaners around the marker into spirals.

5. Have an adult drill holes in the top of the squash for the antennae.

6. Place glow sticks inside when you're ready to display your creation.

squash—a fleshy fruit that grows on a vine in many shapes, sizes, and colors

NOSEY MONSTER

Pick your pumpkin's nose! Choose a pumpkin with the goofiest-looking stem for a nose.

WHAT YOU NEED:

- ❏ a pumpkin with a long stem
- ❏ carving tools
- ❏ a marker
- ❏ a clay sculpting loop
- ❏ plastic fake eyes
- ❏ black **acrylic paint**

1. Turn your pumpkin on its side with the stem "nose" pointing down.

2. Cut an opening in what is now its bottom. Remove the guts.

3. Draw on the face. Use the carving tools to scrape out the mouth area and carve eye sockets.

4. Use the clay sculpting loop to shape the teeth and eye areas. Then carve out the teeth.

5. Stick in plastic eyes. Paint the eyebrows with black paint.

acrylic paint—a type of paint made from chemicals and often used for crafts

DEVILISH DEMON

This pumpkin has a touch of evil in it. Your devilish demon will freak out your visitors.

1. Cut an opening in the bottom of the pumpkin. Remove its guts.

2. Draw on the face, and mark where the horns will go.

3. Cut four small holes for horns. Push the parsnips into the holes from the inside. Use toothpicks to hold them in place.

4. Cut out two eyes, one long nostril slit, and a mouth.

5. Use the clay loop to remove the peel and shape the teeth and eyes.

6. Place a slice of the pepper in the mouth to make a tongue. Hold it in place with toothpicks.

7. Place glow sticks inside when it's ready to display.

BRAIN-SLURPING PUMPKIN

Want to gross out your neighbors? This brain-sucking jack-o'-lantern will do the trick!

WHAT YOU NEED:

- ❏ a large white pumpkin
- ❏ carving tools
- ❏ a small aluminum pan
- ❏ a small orange pumpkin
- ❏ a marker
- ❏ a drill
- ❏ a clay sculpting loop
- ❏ a long bendy straw
- ❏ yellow glow sticks

1. Cut an opening the size of your pan in the top of the large pumpkin. Remove the guts, but keep them.

2. Cut an opening on the side of the small pumpkin. Remove its guts.

Continued on next page

15

3. Draw on the faces. Then carve them. You will need to ask an adult to drill a hole for the small pumpkin's mouth. This hole should be at the bottom of the pumpkin.

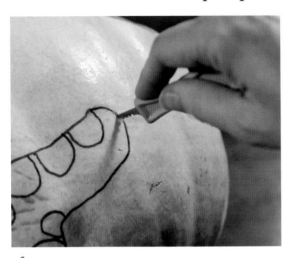

4. Use carving tools to remove the skin from the teeth and eyes. Shape the teeth with the clay loop.

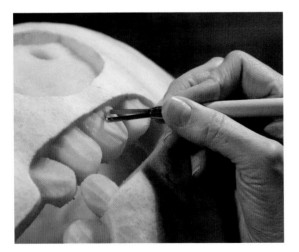

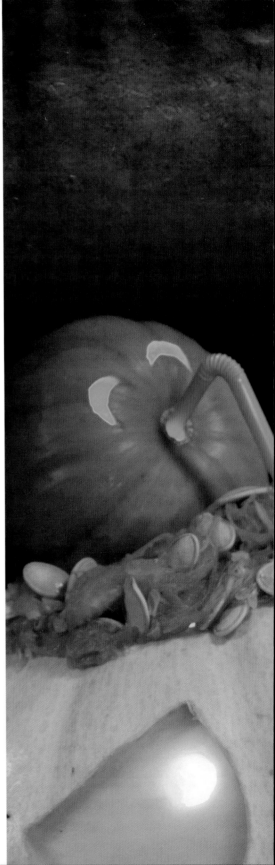

5. Fill the pan with pumpkin guts. Set it in the large pumpkin.

6. Put the small pumpkin on the big one. Stick the straw from small pumpkin's mouth into the large pumpkin's "brains."

7. Add glow sticks to display.

immigrant—someone who comes from one country to live permanently in another country

WART-COVERED CREATURE

Find a gross-looking gourd for this creation. This nasty-looking creature looks like it just crept out of a nearby swamp.

WHAT YOU NEED:

- ❏ a lumpy, wrinkled gourd
- ❏ carving tools
- ❏ a marker
- ❏ drill (optional)
- ❏ 2 fake squishy eyes
- ❏ a clay sculpting loop

1. Cut an opening in the bottom of the **gourd**. Remove its guts, but keep some.

2. Draw on a face. Use the carving tools to remove the skin from the nose and mouth. Cut holes big enough for the eyes. Some gourds are thick. You may want to ask an adult to drill holes for eyes instead of carving them.

3. Squeeze the squishy eyeballs into their **sockets**.

4. Shape the teeth and nose with the clay loop.

5. Hang some of the stringy guts from the teeth, eyes, and nose for a truly gross look.

---

gourd—a fruit with a rounded shape like a squash or pumpkin

socket—a hole or hollow place where something fits in

HOWLING WEREWOLF

Sometimes a pumpkin doesn't need much carving to come to life. This scary werewolf is ready to howl at the moon.

WHAT YOU NEED:

- ❏ polyester stuffing
- ❏ brown spray paint
- ❏ a pumpkin
- ❏ carving tools
- ❏ a marker
- ❏ plastic vampire teeth
- ❏ industrial–strength glue
- ❏ yellow, red, black, and acrylic paints
- ❏ acrylic sealer
- ❏ green glow sticks

1. Have an adult spray-paint strands of stuffing. Let them dry.

2. Cut an opening in the bottom of the pumpkin. Remove its guts.

3. Have an adult spray-paint the pumpkin. Let it dry.

Continued on next page

4. Draw on the face. Cut a mouth opening the size of the vampire teeth. Glue in the teeth.

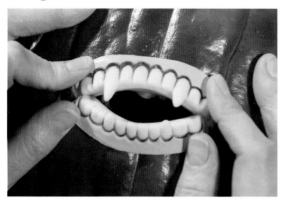

5. Paint the eyes yellow, the nose and lips black, and blood drips red. Let the paint dry.

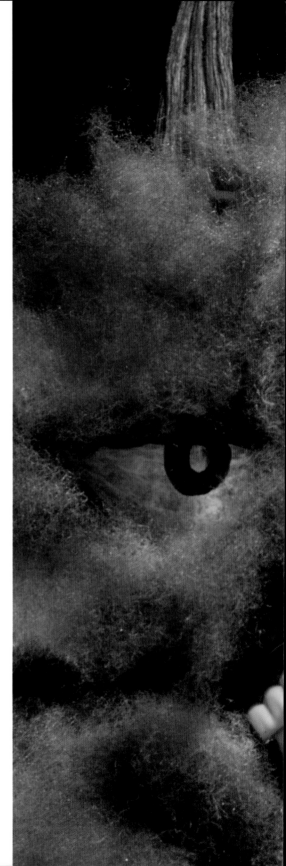

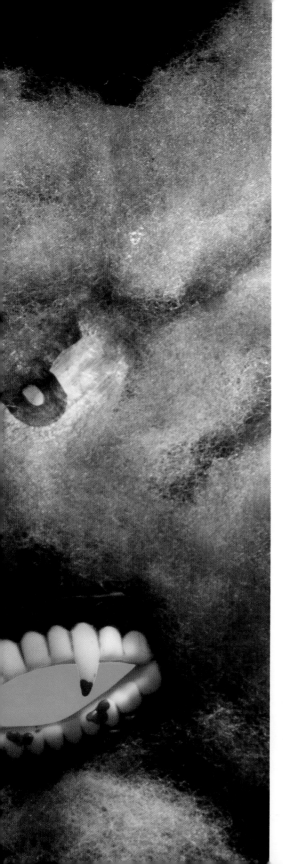

6. Have an adult spray the pumpkin with clear acrylic sealer.

7. With an adult's help, cover your werewolf's face with fur. Glue on long strands of the painted stuffing starting out from the nose. Add more on the forehead and as a mustache. Glue shorter strands next to the eyes and under its mouth.

8. Add glow sticks to display.

SKULL ON A STAKE

Welcome guests with this creepy skull carving.

1. Turn the squash so that the large bulb is at the top.

2. Draw on a face. Cut out the eyes, nose, and a large mouth. Remove the guts through its mouth.

3. Cut a hole in the bottom that is smaller than your stake.

4. Remove the skin from the teeth with a carving tool. Shape the teeth with the clay loop.

5. Pound your stake into the ground. Gently place the skull on the stake.

6. Display the pumpkin with glow sticks and polyester stuffing in its mouth.

Tip:

As days pass, this skull will start to shrivel and look even more dreadful. Add props to your shrunken head to increase the fright factor.

CANNIBAL PUMPKIN

Talk about a jawbreaker! This evil cannibal pumpkin was caught chomping on its next meal.

WHAT YOU NEED:

- ❏ carving tools
- ❏ a large pumpkin
- ❏ a mini pumpkin
- ❏ a marker
- ❏ toothpicks
- ❏ red jelly (optional)
- ❏ orange glow sticks

1. Cut an opening in the bottom of the large pumpkin. Remove its guts.

2. Draw faces on both of the pumpkins. Cut out the faces. Remove the guts.

3. Use carving tools to remove the skin from the teeth of the large pumpkin and the eyes of both pumpkins.

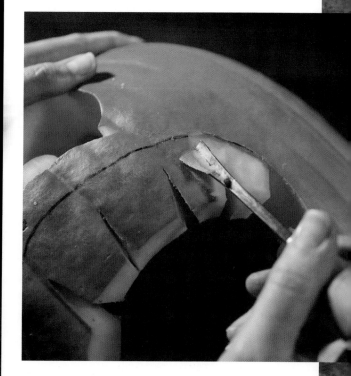

Continued on next page

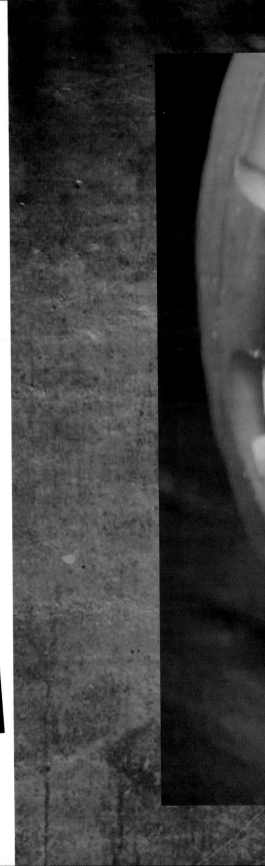

4. Place the mini pumpkin in the large pumpkin's mouth. Hold it in place with toothpicks.

5. For an optional addition of gore, add some red jelly as blood.

6. Add glow sticks to display.

Freaky Fact:

In 2014 Trevor Hunt broke the world's record for fastest pumpkin carving. He carved 109 pumpkins in 1 hour.

GLOSSARY

acrylic paint (uh-KRIH-lik PAYNT)—a type of paint made from chemicals and often used for crafts

aluminum (uh-LOOM-uh-nuhm)—a type of metal

cannibal (KA-nuh-buhl)—something that eats the flesh of its own kind

gourd (GORD)—a fruit with a rounded shape like a squash or pumpkin

immigrant (IM-uh-gruhnt)—someone who comes from one country to live permanently in another country

preserve (pri-ZURV)—to protect something so that it stays in its original condition

socket (SOK-it)—a hole or hollow place where something fits in

squash (SKWAHSH)—a fleshy fruit that grows on a vine in many shapes, sizes, and colors; squashes are related to pumpkins and gourds

READ MORE

Cupp, Lundy. *Realistic Pumpkin Carving: 24 Spooky, Scary, and Spine-Chilling Designs.* East Petersburg, Penn.: Fox Chapel Publishing, 2016.

Hardyman, Robyn. *Origami for Halloween.* Origami Holidays. New York: PowerKids Press, 2016.

Owen, Ruth. *The Halloween Gross-Out Guide.* DIY for Boys. New York: PowerKids Press, 2014.

INTERNET SITES

Use FactHound to find Internet sites related to this book.

Visit *www.facthound.com*

Just type in 9781543530322 and go!

Super-cool stuff! Check out projects, games and lots more at **www.capstonekids.com**

INDEX